Permaculture Gardening For Beginners

The Ultimate Practical Guide To Permaculture Gardening And Permaculture Design

Table of Contents

Introduction

This book contains proven steps and strategies on how to design, build and maintain your own permaculture garden. You will learn to use the principles of permaculture to create a productive, low-maintenance home garden that is environmentally sustainable. No matter how much or how little space you have available, you can grow some of your own food!

Here Is A Preview Of What You'll Learn...

- What permaculture is and how it works
- How to create self-sustaining no-dig garden beds no matter where you live
- What to plant in your garden
- How to control pests and plant diseases without chemicals
- Which plants work well together
- How to use perennials and self-seeding plants to reduce your work load

And much, much more!

Chapter 1 – What is Permaculture?

If you have ever planted a garden, you know the routine. Each spring you dig or till the soil and plant new seeds and seedlings, which grow quickly. Like jungle growth after the clear-cutting of a forest, your tomatoes, cucumbers, beans and lettuce thrive in the disturbed soil of a typical garden.

This style of gardening is obviously productive, but it also creates some problems. When you till the soil, you aerate it, but you also disturb the soil microbes and worms that help to keep it naturally healthy. You also activate the weed seeds in the soil, causing them to germinate and compete with your own. The bare soil dries out quickly and needs to be watered often. If you plant a typical garden with all plants of one kind together in a row, insect pests can easily find your crops and destroy them. In short, the "normal" backyard garden requires you to dig it up and plant it every year, and then keep up with weeding, watering and pest control. If you go away for a couple of weeks in the summer, you may come home to a disaster.

On an industrial scale, the problems are even bigger. As the soil's nutrients get depleted by monoculture farming year after year, farmers become more dependent on chemical fertilizers. Pesticides are used to kill both weeds and insects, but these have side-effects: the chemicals can harm human and animal health, and farmers can end up killing important pollinators along with the insect pests. Runoff even from organic fertilizer can pollute waterways.

Permaculture takes a step back from what has become "traditional" gardening, and tries to learn from nature. Most natural ecosystems do not consist of a monoculture where one species dominates the landscape. There is no such thing as a "good" or "bad" insect or plant – all exist in relation to the rest of the system. In nature, soil does not get tilled and ploughed every spring; insects do not destroy an entire species in a given area (unless an exotic species is accidentally introduced); and nobody weeds or waters the plants. What if people could plant ecosystems instead of crops? What if we could set up the initial conditions so that a productive food garden could grow without constant work on our part? What if we could feed ourselves and take what we need from the natural world without destroying it?

Permaculture is about more than just growing food:

Permaculture is a philosophy of working with, rather than against nature; of protracted and thoughtful observation rather than protracted and thoughtless labor; and of looking at plants and animals in all their functions, rather than treating any area as a single product system.

—Bill Mollison, *Introduction to Permaculture* (1991)

This philosophy has applications in engineering, architecture, water management, and community planning, as well as agriculture and forestry.

Here are some of the key principles of permaculture:

Observe: See what is really happening before you step in and try to change it. When you need to intervene, make small changes and solve problems slowly.

There's no such thing as waste: In a natural system, one organism's waste is food for another organism. Dead trees in a forest become habitat for organisms who, through their life cycles, return nutrients to the soil. If the by-products of our activities are used properly, they do not become pollutants.

Value diversity: Genetic diversity in food crops means less chance of a devastating loss of harvest to disease or pests. Diversity of outlooks and opinions makes a community more resilient to unexpected challenges.

Use renewable resources: Our world is finite, and we simply cannot consume more resources than are available.

Because our need for food creates the biggest and most immediate demands on our environment, agriculture is the obvious area to start using the principles of permaculture.

For much of our history, the vast majority of people were subsistence farmers, and in some of the poorer parts of the world this is still the case. Clearly nobody wants to go back to this model. Some level of large-scale agriculture is needed to feed the world's billions, but there is no reason why many more of us could not be producing some of our own food (and there's plenty of room for reform and more sustainable practices in large-scale agriculture). The beauty of permaculture gardening is that once a system is set up, it doesn't require the same daily labor to maintain that is needed for traditional gardening and subsistence farming. We don't all have to be professional farmers, or even enthusiastic gardeners, in order to take a more active role in growing our own food.

Chapter 2 – Some Permaculture Garden Designs

This book will introduce you to some of the principles of permaculture gardening, and tell you how to create some sustainable gardens wherever you happen to live. Even if all you have is a balcony, you can grow edible plants, and the principles of permaculture can make your garden easier to maintain in the long run.

General Guidelines about Permaculture/No-Dig Gardens

- Make sure you create walkways so you can access the whole garden bed. It's especially important not to compact the soil by stepping on it because you won't be tilling it every spring.
- If you use newspaper in the construction, don't use any glossy supplements as the ink is toxic. Both black and colored inks on regular newsprint are fine.
- Your own urine, diluted 1 part to 9 parts water, can be used to add nitrogen to your garden (if you can't get your head around this, don't worry – there are plenty of other options!) Use this to add nitrogen in

the second layer along with your manure or compost. Don't use human feces unless you have a composting toilet and really know what you're doing.

- For a hügelkultur garden, be careful of where you get your wood. Try to use fallen trees or wood that would otherwise go to waste rather than chopping down trees. Also, don't use treated lumber as it can be toxic.

- Along with finished compost, you can add compostable kitchen scraps directly to the inside layers. Later on you can compost some of your vegetable scraps this way, by simply tucking them under the top mulch layer of your garden.

Building a Sheet Mulch Garden

Sheet mulching uses a series of layers to prepare your garden for planting. The bottom layer acts as a weed barrier, preventing unwanted seeds that are already in the soil from sprouting and growing. The manure, compost and/or topsoil provide plant nutrients (especially nitrogen), and the mulch layer provides carbon and holds in moisture. The result is a garden that will need very little weeding or watering once it is established.

The best time to set up this garden bed is in the late autumn so it can sit over the winter. If you've already missed that opportunity, you can also set it up and wait just a few weeks before planting.

Before you get started, you may want to do a soil analysis of the spot where you want your garden. If your soil is lacking in a particular nutrient, you can supplement it with some of these soil additives:

- Lime to lower acidity
- Gypsum to raise acidity
- Bone meal to add phosphorus
- Glacial rock dust to add trace minerals

A thin layer before you lay down the cardboard is sufficient.

What you'll need

- Cardboard or newspaper
- Compost or manure
- Mulch or straw (avoid black walnut, pine and cedar)
- Topsoil

Instructions

1. Lay out a layer of cardboard or several layers of newspaper over the area where you want your garden. Lay it on top of any existing grass or weeds, without digging or tilling. If there are tall plants, you can trim them down first, but leave the stalks on the ground and don't dig into the soil. Water the cardboard thoroughly.

2. Add a layer of compost or manure to a depth of one or two inches on top of the cardboard. You can also add fresh grass clippings. The purpose of this layer is to add nitrogen to the soil.

3. Add a very thick layer of mulch or straw, about 8 inches thick. You can also use dead leaves or wood shavings, or a combination of all of these materials.

4. Give this layer a good soaking with water.

5. Add an inch or two of topsoil or more compost.

6. Add a final layer of mulch, etc. (about 2 inches). It's best to keep straw out of this layer in case it contains seeds that may sprout and cause problems for you later.

7. Once again, water the whole area thoroughly.

8. If you like, you can plant a cover crop of clover, to help fix nitrogen and speed up the process of breaking down the layers.

The layers in this garden continue to break down over time. You will plant your seeds or seedlings under the top layer of mulch, but eventually the roots will grow through all of the layers and into the natural soil beneath.

Building a Hügelkultur Garden Bed

This style of gardening has been used for a long time in parts of Germany and Eastern Europe. A hügelkultur bed uses large amounts of decomposing wood to keep the garden moist and nourished. Just as in a natural forest, dead wood decomposes and returns nutrients to the soil for other plants to use.

A hügelkultur garden takes a lot of effort to set up, but once it's built it is very low-maintenance. It can go for weeks without being watered because of the moisture trapped in the waterlogged decomposing wood. Over a few years, the logs rot and create air pockets that help to aerate the soil. The decomposing wood creates heat, allowing you to extend your growing season in colder climates. And you can't beat the flavor of fruits and vegetables grown in a hügelkultur bed.

Most people build these as long raised mounds that they can access by simply walking around them. The mounds should be no more than 3 feet wide. If you're ambitious and have understanding neighbours, you can build as high as seven feet, which will enable your garden to go for months without watering. The beds will sink over time as the wood decomposes.

Of course, it's also fine to just build the beds a few feet high, or even to dig a trench and bury the wood a little below ground level (if you do this, include the soil and sods in your nitrogen level.) Some people build them higher over the course of a few years, planting only annuals until the bed is completely established.

What you need:

- Wood (logs, stumps, trees, branches, twigs)
- A nitrogen source (manure, compostable kitchen scraps, bone or blood meal, fresh grass clippings)
- Topsoil and/or compost
- Mulch or straw

Instructions

1. Choose a place to build. If you're building your mound on thick soil, you can dig some of it out and use it as your topsoil layer.
2. For your first layer of wood, choose the biggest pieces and lay them out lengthwise. Continue to build upward into a gradually narrowing mound shape, thoroughly hosing down each layer with water. Use smaller pieces of wood for each layer, finishing with twigs.
3. Add a layer of manure, kitchen scraps, grass clippings etc, filling in the spaces between the branches.
4. Add a 2-inch layer of topsoil and/or compost, and a layer of mulch or straw on top.

Just as with the sheet layer garden, it's best to let this one sit either for a few weeks or (ideally) over the winter. If you like, you can plant a cover crop such as crimson clover. However, if you're anxious to get going or you were late starting, you can plant in this bed right away.

A Permaculture Balcony Garden

Even if the only space you have available is an apartment balcony, you can still grow some of your own food.

The biggest difference between a permaculture container garden and any other kind is the soil preparation. Permaculture views soil as a living, interacting ecosystem rather than just a physical support and nutrient source for your plants. As a permaculture gardener, you cultivate the soil and the soil looks after your plants.

Because a container garden, especially on a balcony, is so isolated from the rest of nature, you need to work a little harder to create living soil. This is why it's best if you can steal a bit of natural soil from a wooded area to help establish soil microbes. You may also need to use inoculants if you grow beans to help them fix nitrogen in the soil. And not surprisingly, you'll have to water more than with a regular outdoor garden bed.

Take a good look at your balcony before you get started. How much sun does it get? You may be able to use reflectors to direct a little more sun towards your growing area. You may also want to grow plants in raised containers to give them more light.

Layering plants and planters is also a good idea. A trellis can support climbing plants that are rooted in the same soil as shorter plants. If your balcony does get a lot of direct sunlight, you can use the taller plants to provide shade for plants that don't do well with too much sun.

What You Need

- Containers with drainage
- Potting soil and/or sand
- If possible, a few cups of natural soil
- Compost
- Mulch

Instructions

1. Fill the bottom of the container with about 6 inches of potting soil, sand, or a combination.
2. Mix in a little of the natural soil. Water well.
3. Add a thin layer of compost, and top with a 4-inch layer of mulch. Water well again.
4. Add a 2 inch layer of compost and water thoroughly.
5. Top with a final 2 inch layer of mulch and water it again.

It's a good idea to plant some clover seeds in the top layer of mulch, and let them get started before you plant anything else. This will help block out weeds and add to the soil's nitrogen levels.

Here is a variation if you want to be able to water less frequently:

Set your container above a deep tray filled with water. There should be some air space between the bottom of the container and the water. Before you fill your container, cut a hole in the bottom just big enough to fit a piece of dead wood into it. This dead wood will stick up above all of the soil levels, and the bottom end of it will be below the water level. Once the wood is waterlogged, it will wick some of the water up into the container. If you like, you can even plant shitake mushroom spores on the log. This setup won't replace watering, but you can get away with watering less often.

Chapter 3 – Planting Your Garden

Now that you've constructed and prepared your garden beds, it's time to start planting.

How to Plant

The process is the same, whether you have a sheet mulch bed, a hügelkultur bed or containers. Dig a small hole through the top layer of mulch. Add a handful of compost and plant your seed or seedling. Try to keep the mulch slightly away from the base of the seedling. Water.

If you have planted a cover crop like clover, you may need to cut it down before planting. Just cut it short and leave the cuttings in place, or bury them under the mulch if you can do so without too much digging.

What to Plant in your Permaculture Garden

You can grow pretty much the same plants you would grow in a conventional garden. Many permaculture gardeners build their gardens around the perennials – fruit trees and bushes as well as a number of vegetables – and self-seeding annuals. After all, the emphasis is on creating a self-sustaining system, so although you can still plant your favorite annuals, they may not be the focal point of your garden.

One typical permaculture garden layout involves a canopy of taller fruit trees; some dwarf fruit trees; berry bushes; perennial vegetables and herbs; and root vegetables. A water feature such as a small pond may also be included. This layering mimics the structure of a natural forest ecosystem. All the components support each other, and you can get a much bigger yield and variety of plants than in a conventional backyard garden. Even if you only have space for one or two fruit trees, you can do a miniature version of this layout.

Fruit Trees

Grow fruits that work in your hardiness zone. If you've got a deep hügelkultur bed, you may even be able to sneak in a tree from a lower zone in a sheltered location, because of the heat from the decomposing wood.

The biggest task associated with fruit trees is prur Permaculture gardeners have found that you don't ever actually have to prune fruit trees as long as they have never been pruned (once you start, you have to continue). If you're trying to grow a tree that's not quite hardy for your zone, not pruning it can help to further insulate the roots as the branches hang down to ground level during winter.

You can build a sheet mulch garden under your fruit trees, with the trees providing shade for plants that need it. Fallen leaves can act as part of your mulch layer, protecting the soil's moisture and providing nutrients as they decompose.

Edible Perennials

- Artichokes – This relative of the thistle is perennial in mild climates. They need a fair amount of water.
- Asparagus – Plant one-year-old crowns to give these a head start. It takes a few years to really establish asparagus, but it's worth it. An asparagus patch will last at least 20 years without replanting.
- Broccoli – One breed of broccoli, Nine Star, can be grown as a perennial.

- Garlic – To grow this as a perennial, pinch off all the buds before they flower, but only harvest the biggest plants. Leave the smaller ones to propagate and spread. If you love garlic scapes (the edible flower bud and stem), grow hardneck garlic.
- Herbs – Chives, lavender, lemon balm, mint, oregano, rosemary, sage, thyme and many other herbs are perennial.
- Lovage – This plant is now unfamiliar to most people, but it's worth getting to know it. Every part of it is edible, and the stems taste a bit like a stronger version of celery. Very easy to grow.
- Raspberries, blackberries, blueberries, currants – Find out which berry bushes do best in your area and plant your favorites. Some of these require annual pruning. You will probably want to rig up some netting around the bushes to avoid feeding the entire crop to the birds.
- Rhubarb –very easy to grow, and makes great pies in spring and early summer. The leaves and roots are toxic, but the stems and early flower buds are both edible.

- Scarlet runner beans – These are perennial in mild climates, and extremely easy to grow as annuals even in places where they can't last the winter.
- Sea kale – Every part of this remarkable plant can be eaten: roots, shoots, stems, leaves and flower heads.
- Sorrel – the leaves of this herb can be eaten in salads or pureed in soups
- Strawberries – plant these near your asparagus and let them spread from year to year.
- Sunchokes – Also known as Jerusalem artichokes, this relative of the sunflower has delicious edible tubers. From time to time, dig up a few tubers and move them to new soil to grow.

Self-Seeding Annuals

Many of the annual plants that you grow will re-seed themselves if you give them a chance. Allow some of your lettuce, radishes and carrots to go to seed without harvesting, and you'll find that some of next year's planting will be done for you. Leave a few beans, tomatoes and peppers on the plants especially near the end of the season. If some of your tomatoes split before you get to them, scatter them throughout the garden instead of removing them.

Open-pollinated (also known as heirloom) varieties work best as self-seeders because they are genetically more diverse to begin with. Plants grown from hybrids, which have been carefully cross-bred to select specific characteristics, will often re-seed as well, but the next generation may be quite different from the original plants.

The goal is to end up with "half-wild" self-seeding annuals that are well adapted to your garden's conditions, resistant to disease and insects, and generally low-maintenance. Some of these may not be very palatable, but you will find many that you love as well.

Annuals

There will likely always be some annuals that you choose to start from scratch every year. Tomatoes and peppers, for example, may not have time to grow from seeds if you have long winters and a short growing season. You may have some favorite hybrids that don't self-seed reliably. And there are some plants that benefit from crop rotation.

Your annuals will require the most day-to-day attention, so when you're planning your garden layout, try to have the annual beds closest to your house.

If you grow annuals in a sheet mulch bed, you may need to add another layer at some point. At the end of the growing season, lay down a few layers of newspaper; top with an inch or two of compost and/or manure, and cover the whole thing with mulch. Give it a good soaking and plant a cover crop if you wish.

Chapter 4 – Growing Potatoes

Growing Potatoes

Potatoes get their own chapter because they are one of the few staple foods that can be grown efficiently in a backyard garden (families don't tend to grow their own wheat, for example). They also present some challenges and cannot be planted simply using the methods outlined earlier in this book.

Potatoes are a favorite crop with home gardeners, partly because commercially-grown commercial potatoes are loaded with pesticides. Potatoes are notoriously prone to disease and insects, mostly because they lack genetic diversity due to being propagated from tubers rather than seeds. All the tubers of a parent plant are genetically identical to the parent and to each other.

Farmers in what is now Peru have been growing potatoes possibly for as long as ten thousand years. They developed thousands of different varieties, and Andean farming villages today still produce dozens of varieties. You can find more genetic diversity in a single Andean potato field than in most of the US put together.

When Europeans first brought potatoes back to their own countries, planting crops from tubers was unheard of. Unaware of the dangers of a lack of diversity, they cultivated a very few varieties of potatoes, and poor people soon discovered how easy it was to grow enough potatoes to feed a large number of people. Potatoes fueled the Industrial Revolution, just as they had fueled the expansion of the Incan Empire.

In Ireland, a whole family could live off a backyard potato patch and the milk of one cow. When a potato blight struck in the 1840s, the genetically identical potato crop of Ireland was defenceless against this disease, and more than a million people died. Not long after, the first chemical pesticides made of arsenic began to appear, and the rest is history.

Clearly potatoes are a good crop for people who want to grow a significant amount of their own food in a small space. Equally clearly, conventional potato gardening involves a lot of digging and maintenance, and it can be hard to control disease and pests.

Here are some permaculture innovations:

Raised Composter/Potato Bed

What you need

- Chicken wire
- Four wooden stakes, at least 3 feet long
- Yard waste, straw, mulch
- Compostable kitchen scraps
- Topsoil and/or finished compost
- Seed potatoes

Instructions

1. Decide how big you want your potato patch to be. Hammer in a wooden stake in each corner, leaving about 2 ½ feet above ground.
2. Construct a 2 1/2 foot tall cage with the wire by cutting it to size and stapling it to the wooden stakes.
3. Fill the cage with straw, compostables, mulch, leaves, grass clippings, etc. to a depth of 2 feet. Water well.

4. Add six inches of topsoil and/or finished compost on top. Plant your seed potatoes in this top layer. Add mulch.

5. When the sprouts appear, draw some of the soil up over them to protect them. When the plants are about 9 inches tall, draw soil around them again to prevent the tubers from turning green when exposed to light. Water as needed.

6. When it's time to harvest your potatoes, cut the wire so that the bed falls apart. You can easily pick through to get your potatoes, and you're left with a pile of finished or almost-finished compost that you can use elsewhere in your garden.

Mulching with Straw

This method allows you to grow potatoes without a lot of back-breaking digging. These potatoes are much less work to harvest, and the mulch helps keep the weeds under control.

1. If you're planting on unprepared soil, loosen it well with a hoe and add a layer of compost. Alternatively, you can start with an already prepared sheet mulch bed or hügelkultur mound.

2. Plant the seed potatoes about 3 inches deep. Cover with a layer of straw and water well.

3. To prevent the wind from blowing away all of your straw, cover it with a mesh or net if necessary. Straw can dry out more quickly than soil, so you may have to put in a little more effort to keep the bed irrigated.

4. Add more layers of straw and other mulch (grass clippings and dead leaves, for example) as the plants get taller. You will need to do this to keep the potatoes in the dark so they don't turn green. Keep the bed well watered but not soaked.

With this method, it is easy to see if your potatoes are ready by just pushing aside some of the mulch and looking at them. It's also possible to harvest a few potatoes from a plant without killing the whole plant. You'll also appreciate not having to use sharp tools to dig out the potatoes (and often damaging them in the process.)

Planting from Seeds

There are a couple of good reasons why potatoes are normally planted from sprouted tubers rather than seeds. The tubers grow quickly, without needing to take the time to germinate. Also, seed-grown potatoes are unpredictable and unreliable in their results: a plant that produces high-quality potatoes may have offspring whose tubers bear no resemblance to the parent's.

Seeds also have their advantages. The biggest is genetic diversity. Tubers are clones of the parent, while seeds combine the genes of two different plants. And for permaculture enthusiasts, unpredictability presents just as many opportunities as problems. Rather than having a cellar full of potatoes that all taste exactly the same, you can have variety. You can save a few of the ones that worked out particularly well and plant them as tubers the following year.

Most available varieties of potato do not even produce fruit and seeds, but you can buy seeds online – look for "true potato seed." Potatoes produce small fruits that look like little tomatoes. You can save these and plant them again, or let the plants re-seed by themselves.

Chapter 5 – Guilds and Harvesting

Companion Planting

The concept of companion planting is central to permaculture. Different plants work together in groups that permaculturists refer to as "guilds." In a guild, each element performs a different function or better yet, multiple functions. The result is a grouping that's stronger and more resilient than any of the individual parts.

One famous example is a North American grouping known as the Three Sisters in which corn, beans and squash are planted together. The corn stalks act as a trellis for the climbing beans; the beans fix nitrogen in the soil, and the squash acts as a living mulch, locking in moisture and crowding out weeds. At the end of the season, the roots are left in the soil and the rest of the plants become mulch for next year's crop.

Another example is the use of non-edible flowering plants in a vegetable garden. Some flowers attract pollinators and predator insects while others such as marigolds repel harmful insects and soil pests such as nematodes. Many permaculture practices also aim to provide habitat that attracts spiders and toads to the garden, both of which eat some of the creatures that feast on your plants.

Research the plants that you want to have in your garden and see which companions are best for them.

Harvesting

Even the way you harvest your plants can contribute to your permaculture guild. The basic principle is to take only what you will use and leave the rest behind as part of the system.

Instead of uprooting cabbages and broccoli, try just cutting out the central edible part. If you leave the roots and part of the stems behind, you often will get a second crop. Common "cut and come again" crops include lettuce, celery, green onions, broccoli, herbs and fennel. Even if the plant does not grow back, the roots will stay in the soil and provide nutrients for future plants. In the case of herbs and lettuce, just remove a few leaves from each plant and the plant will regenerate.

Allow some of your plants to go to seed to provide new plants for next year. Radishes are great for this, because they grow quickly in the spring, out-competing weeds and you some fresh vegetables to munch on while you

)r everything else to grow.

When you harvest beans, corn and other fruiting crops, don't remove the stalks and roots. Just cut them down and leave them as mulch. For root vegetables such as carrots, return the tops of the plants to the soil after you pull out the roots. All of this ensures that the nutrients the plants used in growing remains in the system where it can be used by future plants.

Finally, if you enjoyed this book, then I'd like to ask you for a favor, would you be kind enough to leave a review for this book on Amazon? It'd be greatly appreciated!

Thank you and good luck!

Made in the USA
Monee, IL
12 December 2019